REINCARNATION

TEACHINGS OF THE ORDER OF CHRISTIAN MYSTICS

THE "CURTISS BOOKS" FREELY AVAILABLE AT

WWW.ORDEROFCHRISTIANMYSTICS.CO.ZA

REINCARNATION

Transcribed by
HARRIETTE AUGUSTA CURTISS
and
F. HOMER CURTISS, B.S., M.D.
Founders of
THE ORDER OF CHRISTIAN MYSTICS
and
AUTHORS OF THE "CURTISS BOOKS"

2015 EDITION

REPUBLISHED FOR THE ORDER BY
MOUNT LINDEN PUBLISHING
JOHANNESBURG, SOUTH AFRICA
ISBN: 978-1-920483-27-2

INTRODUCTION

So many have asked for a brief and direct, though comprehensive treatment of a subject that especially concerns all thinking people—namely Reincarnation—that it becomes almost imperative that we, The Universal Religious Fellowship, Inc., issue such a treatise. However, instead of writing one, it occurs to us that since we have not found any treatment of this vital subject in clearer or more definitely organized form than in the four pamphlets issued some time ago by Dr. F. Homer Curtiss, our late beloved teacher and friend, we could do no better than to combine these four booklets into one, and put this valuable information forth for the blessing of all who read it.

"Ministers of Christ and Stewards of the Mysteries of God."

1 Corinthians 4 vs. 1

COPYRIGHT 2015

BY
MOUNT LINDEN PUBLISHING

First Published in 1949

CONTENTS

REINCARNATION

PART I.

"Our birth is but a sleep and a forgetting;
The Soul that rises with us, our life's star,
Hath had elsewhere its setting
And cometh from afar,"
Intimations of Immortality, Wordsworth.

"Think not, when'er material forms expire,
Consumed by wasting age or funeral fire,
Aught else can die; souls, spurning death's decay,
Freed from their old, new tenements of clay
Forthwith assume, and wake to life again."
Metamorphoses, Ovid, Book 15, line 156.

THE DOCTRINE

THIS BOOK is not written to convince the skeptics with long arguments and masses of evidence, as there are nearly fifty more or less elaborate volumes and countless articles on the subject available for those who honestly wish to investigate the subject seriously, wherein all phases are treated. We simply set forth our own interpretations of the Law of Reincarnation to give you a clear understanding of the doctrine, clarify disputed points, and to summarize briefly the best available concepts of the subject from many sources.

THREE THEORIES

There are three main theories which attempt to account for the appearance of man on Earth. The materialistic theory is that man is the product of a blind and purposeless evolution, and that his mind—and Soul if such is admitted—is the result of the chemical and molecular activity going on within the body. With the cessation of those activities the body dies and the body and mind—and Soul—disintegrate and disappear forever.

The one life theory holds that each Soul is created brand new by God and enters die body at the time of birth. On this basis the Soul is a slave to a heredity and environment that is not of its own choosing and with which it had nothing to do. According to this theory, at death the Soul remains in the grave "until the last trump," when it is released to pass into purgatory or into heaven or into a hell of everlasting torment.

The third theory is that of reincarnation or the repeated incarnations of the same Soul in one body after another from time to time in various eras.

FACTS EXPLAINED

The supreme test of any theory is: How completely does it explain the facts? Reincarnation explains apparently discordant and irreconcilable phenomena, the inequality of life, the apparent injustice of God, the great differences in personality, from the idiot to the child prodigy and the genius, and assures the certainty of future lives here on earth in which to correct our mistakes, right our wrongs and attain our cherished ambitions and ideals. This removes all fear of death as the certainty of the coming of spring removes the fear of winter.

THE DOCTRINE

Reincarnation is a simple doctrine which is a natural corollary to that of the immortality of the Soul. Briefly, it gives the reasons for, the method and the proof of the repeated, cyclic embodiments on Earth in human form, of the same Spiritual Being or individual Soul. In thus incarnating *you do not become someone else* but are *always yourself*, but manifesting through various human bodies from age to age, just as you dress in different clothes at different seasons of the year. As the most sacred of the Hindu scriptures puts it: "As a man throweth away old garments and putteth on new, even so the dweller in the body, having quitted its old mortal frames, entereth into other which are new."[1]

These new garments make you appear outwardly quite different, yet you are always yourself no matter how many outer garments become worn out and are discarded incarnation after incarnation. Your body is merely your outer garment which you don in order to manifest in this material world. When you are through using it you discard it and withdraw to your home in the higher worlds whence you came. After a period of rest and assimilation of your life's experience you don another body for use during another "day" of experiences in the material world. It is not your present personality—perhaps called "John Smith"—which reincarnates, but the Spiritual Self which animated "John Smith" which is reborn in a new body. The incarnating Ray is the spiritual thread on which all the transient personalities are strung.

The reincarnation of man is as simple and natural as the reincarnation of Nature in the Spring. And rebirth is no more a miracle than is birth.

TRANSMIGRATION

Opposed to *reincarnation* is the repulsive doctrine of *transmigration* of Souls or the incarnation of the Soul in the body of some lower animal. Although held by numbers of the less educated and superstitious Asiatics, this doctrine is a fallacy; for once having reached the human stage of unfoldment, no body less evolved than the human would have the centers and faculties necessary to accommodate and give expression to a human Soul. A pint cup cannot hold a quart. The lesser can never contain the greater. No doubt this doctrine arose because the cultivation of gross animal traits in this life will carry those qualities over into the next incarnation. The glutton will look like a pig, a schemer like a fox, a miser like a vulture, etc.

---

[1] *The Bhagavad Gita*, Chapter ii.

TESTIMONY OF THE AGES

Aside from the fact that this doctrine most satisfactorily solves the problems and *includes all the facts* of our life here on Earth, how else do we know that the doctrine is true? 1st, there is the testimony of the ages. No doctrine or theory can survive critical examination and application from age to age if it is not founded on truth. Theories of science, religion and philosophy arise, flourish for a time, then pass away, but reincarnation eternally remains. In fact, it reaches back beyond recorded history. It is found in the most ancient writings of Egypt, Babylonia, India, Greece, China, Japan, even in Atlantis and Lemuria. Alexander found it among the Gymnosophists of India, Caesar among the Druids of Gaul, and Herodotus among the Egyptians and the Magi of Persia. It was also taught in the mystery schools of Eleusis, Baccus and Isis.

TESTIMONY OF TODAY

Reincarnation is believed in today by more than two-thirds of all mankind, approximately 750 millions in the Orient and over 10 millions in the Occident. But as these numbers include great masses of the uneducated, the mere fact of numbers is not convincing. But when we find the greatest minds of *age after age* following this doctrine it merits our greatest respect. Among spiritual teachers it was taught by Krishna, Buddha, Confucius, Laotsze and Jesus. Among the ancient philosophers, Pythagoras, Plato, Plotinus, Hermes, Proclus, Iamblicus, Porphory and Hirocles. Among the early Church Fathers, Origen, Ammonius Saccus, Justin Martyr, Philo Judeus, Clemens Alexandrinus, Arnobius, Pamphilius, Bruno, St. Bonaventure, St. Francis and St. Gregory, etc. Among later philosophers, Schopenhauer, Lessing, Swedenborg, Hagel, Leibnitz, Boehme, Herder, Fitchte, Descartes, Voltaire, More, etc. Among great authors, Balzac, Victor Hugo, George Sand, Gautier, Sardou, Goethe, Bacon, Scott, Shelley, Flammarion,

Poe, Haggard, Corelli, Coleridge, Franklin, Emerson, Ghandi, Tagore, Henry Ford, etc. Thus the fact that we have the *almost universal testimony* of the greatest and most acute minds the human race has produced throughout the ages to testify to the truth of the Law of Reincarnation, should have great weight with us.

LAW OF CYCLES

The Law of Cycles rules the world, for all manifestation takes place in cycles. Day and night, summer and winter, birth, death and rebirth follow one another in endless succession. First there is expression and manifestation, then withdrawal, assimilation and growth. The tree clothes itself with a body of leaves. This body dies in winter but the tree returns into manifestation *in a new body* of leaves in the next spring. It is the same tree, but with an entirely new body. The butterfly grub dies as the chrysalis is formed, but it is the same entity that is reborn in the entirely different body of the butterfly. The body is no more you than the caterpillar is the butterfly or the grub which enabled the butterfly to manifest. The water-breathing tadpole is reincarnated in the entirely different body of the air-breathing frog, and the wriggling larva reincarnates in the entirely different body of the mosquito. Your life here on Earth is but one summerperiod or "day-at-school" for the Soul. Just as it takes many summer-periods of expression, or incarnations, to perfect the oak, so does it take many summer-periods of expression, or incarnations, to perfect the Soul's expression on Earth.

LAW OF CONSERVATION OF ENERGY

Reincarnation is a perfect illustration of the scientific conception of the Law of the Conservation of Energy. This law shows that a cause once set in motion must have its resultant effect. Hence, no effort, whether for good or evil, but has its results: for no energy is ever lost. Only its form of expression may be changed. The energies generated in one season or one life cannot be obliterated by death, but must find expression in a subsequent season or life. New growth comes forth on the twigs of last year's growth. It does not have to repeat the last season's growth, but has it to start with, build upon and add to.

Soul-force, like all other forms of energy, is likewise conserved. The Soul that has longed and struggled for a desired end, finding its realization cut off by the death of its body, does not lose the fruit of its labor, self-denial and sacrifices. The energy thus generated will accompany it and so affect and modify the next incarnation as to continue the expression of its aim until perfected. Thus the Soul *loses nothing* and *escapes from nothing* it has generated. Nor does it have to repeat the lessons it has already learned. *It brings back* all the talents and attainments it has slowly gained through growth, and builds them into the new personality as *inherent faculties* with which to start the new life.

Innate likes and dislikes, tastes, impulses, fears and even ingrained habits are brought over from the past. Those who fear to enter caves or tunnels may have lost their lives underground in a past life. Those who fear water or ships may have been drowned in the past. Those who love mountains or even deserts, or long to live in some place they have never seen in this life probably had a happy former life in those surroundings. In fact you bring over at least half the traits of your present personality; all those that you have not developed in this life. If one could see your picture from the last life, anyone would recognize your face.

LAW OF CAUSE AND EFFECT

All manifestation is under Cosmic Law and the Law of Cause and Effect governs all expression. Whatever appears to spring suddenly into being seemingly without reason, must nevertheless have an adequate cause, even if as unrecognized as the unseen vapor that condenses into clouds of rain or snow. All attainments are gained only through the slow Law of Growth, cell by cell. The seemingly spontaneous and miraculous attainments of precocious children and geniuses must be the results of the slowly acting Law of Growth. Where and when? Where else could the cause of this effect be generated but in previous lives? Your being *born with* your innate characteristics and talents, also your obvious shortcomings, must be the result of causes *you set up* before your birth and must be personally related to you. For your talents, traits and powers are not the sum of those of your parents, but are yours. Where and when were they set up? Naturally not in heaven, but by you only in some previous life. For you are the *mathematical result* of the causes you set up and the growth attained by your efforts or lack of effort in past lives. Progress is made by overcoming the practical difficulties of our everyday lives, not by running away from them.

INFANT PRODIGIES

Infant prodigies manifest their amazing talents even before their brains are fully developed. The ability of Mozart to play the piano at two years of age, write a sonata at four and an opera at eight cannot be explained by heredity. Joseph Hoffman gave such marvelous improvisations upon themes suggested without notice that he was considered a master of the piano at the age of ten. In fact, many consider him a reincarnation of Mozart.

The mentally deficient negro boy, Blind Tom, never had a musical lesson but could accurately reproduce the most difficult music after hearing it played but once. The uneducated shepherd-boy, Zerah Colburn, at the age of eight could perform such marvelous mathematical feats as mentally extracting the cube root of numbers in hundreds of millions and the square root of numbers containing six figures. He instantly gave the correct number of minutes in 48 years! Pascal, at the age of two, demonstrated mathematical problems with diagrams. At six he wrote the most learned treatise on conic sections that had appeared for ages. Young read fluently at two years of age, and at eight had a thorough knowledge of six languages. William Hamilton began the study of Hebrew at three and at thirteen knew thirteen languages!

The great Hindu sage, Sankaracharya, wrote his great commentary on the *Vedas* at the age of twelve and it still stands today as the greatest masterpiece of its land. The saint, Ramakrishna, was born so spiritually unfolded that he entered the highest state of spiritual consciousness, *Samadhi*, at the age of four. And the boy Jesus was able to astonish the learned masters at the temple in Jerusalem at the age of twelve. These prodigies must have been the result of causes which cannot be accounted for by heredity and environment, as their great talents were not possessed by their parents, their ancestors or by the other children of the same family. Obviously, *the only explanation* is that they were attainments brought over from previous lives.

The attempt to explain the amazing talents of both precocious children and geniuses by either their horoscopes or by psychic control by some ancient discarnate astral personality, does not explain the facts. Twins born so nearly at the same minute that the difference in time could have had only a trifling effect on their horoscopes, should therefore have almost exactly the same characteristics. But the fact is that they may differ widely in size, color of hair and eyes as well as in sex and in character.

A genius whose talents were manifested only when overshadowed — if not actually obsessed — by an astral entity would lead such a Dr. Jekyl and Mr. Hyde life as to clearly reveal the obsession. Also such entities are usually anxious to reveal their names and claim the credit, while the genius insists that he be recognized as the creator of the results. Only reincarnation can explain all the facts.

THE LAW OF RECOGNITION

Upon meeting certain people for the first time why do you often feel that you know them well, as though they were old friends? When you meet others for the first time why do you feel a sudden aversion to them, even though they may be cultured and charming and you know nothing at all about them? In both instances it is because of the relationships you had set up with them; strong ties of either love or dislike made with them in a past life. Similarly, when you visit a city or see a landscape for the first time you feel that you have been there before, and in some instances you know your way among the streets and can even recognize a certain house as being the one in which you had lived once upon a time. Why is your interest in a particular historical personage so intense that you so thrill at seeing his or her picture, or even upon having the name mentioned, that you think you must have been that character? It is because in a past life you were either personally closely associated with that person or had made him your ideal or had identified yourself with his party or cause. Reading about him revives the old memories and feelings.

THE LAW OF JUSTICE

The Law of eternal justice demands reincarnation to explain the great inequalities of birth and condition, for these cannot be explained on the one life theory without making God a monster of injustice. We cannot conceive of God as being unjust. And yet if all Souls are created new and are scattered out over the world haphazardly to incarnate for the first time at birth, then justice demands that all be given equal opportunities and environments. Why should a God of love and mercy afflict the many and favor the few? Why should He create some born diseased or crippled and others healthy and strong; some dying in youth, others in old age; some living in peace and happiness, others in sorrow and tragedy; some with brilliant minds, others imbecile?

If God creates them so unequal and then abandons them to the influence of heredity and circumstances with which they had nothing to do, instead of guiding them to health and happiness, then He would be less considerate and more unjust and unloving than human parents. The wretch who is born of criminal or drunken parents, in the slums where neither health nor virtue are possible, and foredoomed to a life of want and woe; and the genius who is born with every advantage of wealth, education and refinement, have both created causes in past lives which make it impossible for them to be born under any other conditions. You are rewarded not *for* what you have done, but *by* it.

GOD NOT RESPONSIBLE FOR EVIL

Certainly God could not create evil nor create Souls only to make them suffer. But all becomes clear and just when we realize that God is not responsible either for the parents and their heredity and environment, nor for the character and talents of the children. For all the inborn qualities and their physical setting are not a gift of grace from some capricious, whimsical and unjust deity, but are the mathematically exact results of *the causes those Souls set up* in previous lives. The Law of Justice, as defined by Jesus—"Whatsoever a man soweth, that shall he also reap. . . . not one jot or tittle shall in anywise pass from the law until all be fulfilled"—demands that we reap the results of what we sow. And since mercifully we do not have to reap all the good and all the evil in one short life, we must be reborn again and again to reap the results here on the plane where they were created. For you cannot sow a crop in one field and reap it in another, but only in the field where it was sown.

A PHILOSOPHIC NECESSITY

Reincarnation explains all the objections to survival brought in the name of logic, and removes the challenges brought by materialism against idealism. The presence of evil in the world cannot be explained or accounted for by either materialism or divine providence. Reincarnation shows that evil is created by man through his ignorance, mistakes or wilfulness, so naturally he must reap the results of the causes he has set up, *not as punishment* but in exact justice. Thus evil is a whip which goads you by its painful reactions to correct the error and so to progress. Evil measures a lack of unfoldment and is therefore relative and transitory and can be neutralized and paid off. Hence evil is bound to diminish as mankind slowly progresses toward mastery.

Reincarnation is not a mere theory or probability, nor is it revelation. It is a general *law of manifestation* embracing all life. It is the key to many psychological enigmas not otherwise explainable. It is based on positive evidence and demonstration, and *has many physical proofs*, as we shall see later on.

One season of expression and growth is too short to manifest the perfection of the oak. One life-expression on Earth is too short to manifest the perfection of the Soul. Just as you are learning how to make the most of life, you have to leave it incomplete and pass on. The absence of high qualities and attainments now shows the need for their cultivation in a subsequent life. Hence, after a period of rest and assimilation, *you desire to return* to complete your task. But you have the satisfaction of knowing that suffering bravery endured now produces patience and fortitude in the next life. Hardships overcome now produce strength and courage in the future. Self-denial develops the will, and the industrious worker is now sowing the seeds of greatness and plenty in the next life. The wealthy sluggard of today may be a beggar in the next

life, a domineering person may return as a slave or servant. A
selfish and frivolous woman of fashion may return as a servant,
but with the same habits and tastes. Misuse of or squandering
of wealth, or even taking religious vows of poverty to enter
convents or monasteries in a past life, necessitates a lack of
wealth or even poverty in this life. Cultural tastes cultivated
and acquired now will bear fruit as innate refinement and good
taste in future lives.

SCIENTIFICALLY ACCEPTABLE

It is scientifically acceptable because it is not a religious
or metaphysical revelation, but a logical probability which
has now been *scientifically proved*. It agrees with our actual
scientific knowledge and contradicts none of it. It agrees with
natural history, astronomy, geology, palaentology, comparative
anatomy and physiology. It reveals the "unknown factors" in
evolution that are more powerful than heredity, natural se-
lection and environment. It explains the mental and psychic
inequalities even between homologous or identical twins, and
the enormous paradoxical differences between physical and
psychical heredity. It explains the problem of cryptomnesia or
the subconscious memory of past lives revealed under hypnosis
or in trance. It abolishes the need for bizarre hypotheses of
"unperceived causes" and "obscure influences" which cannot
be verified.

IT IS MORALLY SATISFYING

Reincarnation is morally satisfying, as it eliminates injustice from God and from life. It shows that immanent justice
does not depend upon a whim of Deity, but is the result of
the universal Law of Cause and Effect. Thus there is no need
for supernatural intervention. And there are, therefore, no everlasting torments or punishments without end. In the astral
world after death, in the lower realms called "purgatory," you
do suffer from remorse as you look over the moving picture

film of your past life, for on it is recorded not only your acts, but every thought, word and deed, and you can see all your many mistakes and should learn your lessons from them. And naturally you are anxious to come back and correct them. But there you do not remember previous incarnations any more than when here.

You also suffer in your astral body the effects of all the destructive forces you have generated which you have not worked out or neutralized by good thoughts and deeds before death. You continue to suffer from such destructive forces, not forever, but until the amount accumulated has spent itself. Sincere repentance, prayer and a desire to repay and to progress spiritually, gradually purge you from such forces and permit you to ascend into the higher realms. Thus there is no punishment by God, only a reaping of some of the effects of what you yourself have sown. The actual final adjustment must take place in the next life with the other Souls involved.[2] All must be equalized and ended *by your own efforts* one incarnation after the other. There is then no condemnation for the less advanced, for you also are not as advanced as you might have been if you had worked harder.

It reveals *your personal responsibility* for your conditions. Thus it incites to sincere repentance and definite work and accomplishment, not only individually but collectively for the good of all. It inculcates *tolerance* for the mistakes of others through understanding; *brotherhood* through realization; *co-operation* through gratitude; *love* through compassion; *kindness and sympathy* through suffering, and *service to others* as others have helped you.

Part II will explain why, how, when and where you incarnate.

---

[2] For details see *Realms of the Living Dead*, Curtiss.

WHY AND HOW

PART II

"None sees the slow and upward sweep
By which the Soul from life-depths deep
Ascends,—unless, maybe, when free,
With each new death we backward see
The long perspective of our race,
Our multitudinous past lives trace."
                    A Record, William Sharp.

F YOU are truly a spiritual being and one with God in the
spiritual world, why should you come down to Earth and
so terribly limit the expression of your Spiritual Self by
embodying yourself in matter through incarnating in a human-animal body? We have already explained[1] that it is your
destiny to learn by experience how to manifest your Divinity
in *all* planes and in *all* worlds, even in this dense and unre-
sponsive physical world. The physical body is therefore the
most important of all your bodies—your four bodies being
the physical, astral, mental and spiritual—for only through
it can you complete your mission to manifest your Spiritual
Self here on Earth.

REASONS FOR REINCARNATION

But since the Cycle of Necessity requires you to manifest
as much of your Spiritual Self as you have learned to express
through the body of flesh; you may ask why should you thus
incarnate again and again?

1. Because one life is far too short for you to gain the experience in matter necessary for you to fulfill your destiny.[2]
You-are eager to carry out your unfulfilled plans and desires
of the past life.

2. You come back to learn the next major lesson needed to
round out your character and add its qualities to your unfolding

---
[1] For Details see *Why Are We Here?* Curtiss.
[2] For details as to the fate of the suicide see *Realms of the Living Dead*, Curtiss, 151-2.

spiritual growth. In each incarnation you learn certain major and minor lessons. After assimilating them and building them into character, since this Earth is the Plane of Demonstration where all growth must be proved, after ascending out of earth conditions, you naturally desire to incarnate again to be tested so as to *prove through trial* that you have actually built the lessons of the past life into your character and can demonstrate it—through new methods—by passing the same tests successfully the next time.

3. You return to unfold the next spiritual quality or power needed to take your next step in accomplishing your great mission of becoming a Lord of Creation "to have dominion over every living thing that creepeth upon the Earth," by perfectly manifesting your Spiritual Self in earth conditions. To accomplish this you must train the animal self to respond to die guidance of, and express, your Spiritual Self.

4. You return to work out and redeem the results of past mistakes, reap the rewards of your good deeds, and complete the good plans left unfinished in the last life. Thus as you conquer and progress here and now you can make yourself *whatever you wish to be* in the next incarnation. Through kindness to others you will reap happiness in your next incarnation.

5. You return to be with the ones with whom you set up strong ties of love, affection and comradeship, or to neutralize, redeem and secure forgiveness for the enmities and hatreds set up with others. Since hate is the most binding force next to love, be sure to "agree with thine adversary quickly whilst thou art in the way with him" or you will be bound to him closely in the next life until you have worked out the inharmony.

6. You return to do your part in the redemption of matter from the curse of impurity and inharmony which the sins of mankind have placed upon the lower kingdoms and even upon the atoms of the ground you walk on. For in proportion to the degree that you embody and radiate the currents of peace, love, harmony and joy from the Divine Self within, the radio-activity of those spiritual forces purify, uplift and redeem the atoms of your bodies and all the atoms of matter you contact. Your spiritual radiations also uplift and advance the evolution of the lower kingdoms through your understanding, kind and sympathetic treatment of them. Thus do you become an active worker in the redemption of the Earth by radiating the Christ-force from within. Through man came sin into the world and by him must it be redeemed, not through his own power but by the use of the power of the Christ flowing through him.

7. You must continue to return until you learn how to mould and use matter so as to complete your mission of building up a form so perfectly developed that its centers and faculties will permit the expression of the Spiritual Self as perfectly as the limitations of matter will permit. But you must also train the human-animal personality to respond to that spiritual guidance willingly and harmoniously and gladly, subordinating its will to the will of the indwelling Spirit,

8. Even after you have reached full Mastery and no longer need to return to Earth for your own advancement, you may voluntarily return out of love and compassion so that you may teach, relieve suffering or otherwise help your less advanced fellowmen, as do so many great teachers of mankind. Also many advanced Souls return to incarnate in backward or col-ored races to advance their development, as did Booker T. Washington and Dr. George Washington Carver, etc.

MAJOR AND MINOR INCARNATIONS

Incarnations run in cycles of seven. There are three major incarnations, during which you work chiefly to accomplish the main mission for which you came to Earth. In between these major incarnations are four minor ones. In these you work out minor details of the major step you did not complete in the past life and correct the mistakes made. Thus you clear the way for greater advance in the next major incarnation. In the major incarnations you rise to the greatest heights your degree of spiritual unfoldment permits, and may have a distinguished personality. In the minor incarnations, since you are only working out minor details, you may have a very insignificant personality and position in life.

PECULIARITIES EXPLAINED

If no strong ties have been set up, almost any parents in the general environment with the needed unfoldment would do. Parents who strongly object to having children cannot expect a very advanced Soul to come in where it was not wanted, so they often have to put up with an undeveloped Soul who wants a body so badly that it is willing to push in where it is not wanted. And this resentment or even antagonism is often plainly exhibited by the child after birth. If the parents—especially the mother—are indifferent or resentful there may be a fight between several low-type entities to get possession of the body. This struggle may be so great as to affect the mothers mind and cause "puerperal insanity" until the child is born. A child born from a true love union is usually quite superior to one born of either mere passion or when one parent is indifferent or especially if filled with resentment, disgust or loathing.

On the other hand, by holding high ideals the parents can draw to them the highest type or most advanced Soul to which they can affinitize and attract to their environment. Often, however, they may have to give a body to some less advanced Soul with whom they have made strong karmic ties in the past. And this may be a cripple or mental defective or even an imbecile.

"CHANGELINGS"

A change in the Soul incarnating may also take place *after birth*, usually before seven years of age. Thus the Soul who gains ultimate possession of the body may, in rare cases, be quite different from the one who was born in it. This second Soul is called a "changeling." This usually takes place when the family conditions are so inharmonious that the advanced Soul which had incarnated could not stand those conditions and so withdrew and allowed a lower type to take its place. This sometimes happens over night

In the case of the suicide,[3] since the Soul has neither finished out its cycle of life nor prepared to progress in the higher realms, it remains earth-bound until its cycle is up and death would have occurred normally.

LAW OF SEX

Some writers hold that you incarnate first in one sex and then in the other. Others teach that you incarnate seven times in one sex and then seven times in the opposite sex. This is said to be necessary so that the Soul may learn the lessons of both sexes. But our teaching is that the masculine ray of the Spiritual Self—"male and female created He them" (*Genesis i, 27*)—always incarnates in a male body and the feminine ray in a female body, with certain exceptions. Since by their union on Earth—"they twain shall be one flesh" (*Genesis ii, 24, Matthew xix, 5*)—each learns the lessons of the other by this intimate contact. The man must develop the feminine qualities of love, compassion, tenderness, sympathy and intuition, while the woman must develop the masculine qualities of courage, will-power, reason, logic and executive ability.

---
[3] See *Letters from the Teacher, I*, Curtiss, 151.

EXCEPTIONS

The exception occurs when one refuses to learn the lessons of the other, violates their sacred relationship or so mistreats the other that a negative Karma is created which necessitates an incarnation in the body of the opposite sex to learn its lessons by experience instead of by the normal way of association. In these exceptional cases of "mis-fit sexes" the difference between the sex of the incarnating Ray and the sex of its body is so marked that it can be recognized at a glance, often as far as across the street. The "sissy" or effeminate man, and the domineering, masculine type of women—often with a distinct mustache and masculine hands and feet—are examples. Such men prefer foppish dress, have effeminate voices and ways, while such women prefer mannish clothes—we know one who has for years had a police license to wear entire male clothing and pass as a man—and usually have masculine voices, ways, etc.

"MIS-FIT MATES"

Such "misfit incarnations" are usually very unhappy, as no one seems to understand them and they cannot understand themselves. They often meet their true mates and fall deeply in love, but find themselves tragically in bodies of the same sex. This explains why two women fall in love with each other or two men are inseparably attached. This often leads to a beautiful life-long relationship. But if sex relations are attempted perversion naturally results. Our explanation also shows why perverts are homosexual. A number of our students in misfit bodies have come to us in despair—one on the verge of suicide—over their strange and unhappy condition, only to have things happily straightened out by our almost obvious explanation which they had been unable to find elsewhere.

PARENTS FURNISH THE BODY ONLY

Parents furnish only the body, with its family heredity, and the environment. They do not furnish the Soul, the character or even the mind, although the *type of brain* furnished for the mind of the incarnating Soul to use does modify its expression, just as a colored glass modifies the light that passes through it, or as a violin virtuoso is limited in expression by the character of the violin he is obliged to use. The character of the incarnating Soul also modifies the disposition and often the health of the mother, making her happy or cross and irritable, while she is carrying it. This often varies markedly with different children in the same family before their birth.

HOW YOU INCARNATE

Since God is infinite He has no limitation, hence He can have no form. He manifests as a Divine Outshining, an illimitable Radiance. To manifest in the worlds of form He projects individualized Rays of Himself—your Spiritual self—to achieve a definite destiny. Through this Cycle of Necessity your Spiritual Self must learn how to "do the will of the Father on Earth even as it is done in heaven." Hence he must build up a limiting vehicle of expression or body through which to manifest in each world of form.

MENTAL BODY

Responding to the Decree of Manifestation, your Spiritual Self in turn projects from the spiritual world into the mental world a reflection of its Egoic or Causal Body. This forms your mental body or the ideal type of the perfect body you desire. This perfect pattern is then modified by the forces concentrated in the mental permanent atom, which contains the essence of all the mental attainments—also faults—developed in the previous incarnation. The result is by no means the perfect mental body you desired, but it is the best you can have in view of the limitations the last personality generated in the last life. This mental body is composed of the substance of the mental world whose atoms are called "mentoids" or "psychoids."

ASTRAL BODY

Your Spiritual Self then projects a pattern of the mental body into the astral world where it is embodied in astral matter. There the astral body is modified by the astral permanent atom, making it somewhat like but different from the astral body of the previous life. This releases the residue of the forces of the desires, passions and other emotions you experienced in the last incarnation, and thus embodies them in the new personality. As a child you manifest the same mental and emotional traits—both good and bad—you had developed in the past, modified by the family heredity. This accounts for the otherwise inexplicable innate impulses, peculiar tendencies, unconscious habits, favorite pursuits, preferences, fears, phobias, prejudices and antipathies, as well as the unaccountable Soul-stirring friendships between new acquaintances so often manifested before they could have been acquired in this life.

Infancy thus brings to Earth not a blank scroll to be inscribed only with the events of this life, but a scroll bearing the net results of all your past lives. The record of this life will be but the latest page in the history of your manifestation on Earth.

YOU CHOOSE YOUR PARENTS

Once the cyclic time chosen for your incarnation has arrived you are caught in the downward vortex of embodiment and are magnetically attracted to the general environment—race, country, locality, etc.—whose characteristics will give you the best field in which to work out your problems. You then await the zodiacal and planetary conditions most favorable for accomplishing the chief purpose of your incarnation. You do not have certain characteristics because you were born in a certain zodiacal sign and under certain planetary configurations; you are born under those conditions because you already have certain characteristics which affinitize you to those conditions. The astrological environment at the time of birth is determined largely by degree of unfoldment, the desires and the Karma of the Soul.

A fish desires water, a bird the air and the gopher the earth because those are the environments which furnish the conditions necessary for their evolution. Thus the astral atmosphere at the time of conception and birth—as determined by the convergence of the planetary rays—represents the environment best suited to your spiritual evolution. The ancient axiom is, "The stars *impel* but do not *compel*."

Therefore do not blame astrological conditions for either your success or failure. They do have an influence, just as do the sunshine and the rain, but they simply act upon qualities of character already present or absent. It rests with you how you react to them; for another axiom is, "The wise man rules his stars, the fool obeys them."

Within the environment to which you are thus drawn you are then attracted to the parents whose characteristics and heredity will give you the type of body and environment you desire. Usually the parents are those with whom you have set up strong ties in the past. For your further growth and unfoldment must progress from the point where it left off. Thus you choose your parents, not for an easy life, but from the Soul standpoint of love, justice and spiritual progress.

The more advanced Souls—under the guidance of their Mentor or Guardian Angel, and within the limits imposed by their Karma—choose the parents they wish, well knowing the Karma of the past and also the limitations their heredity and environment will impose. But in spite of any such drawbacks they choose that avenue of incarnation as the best one through which to work out their problems, make their desired advance and attain the destined position in life to which their Karma entitles them.

If the parents chosen fail to give them a body they have to take the next best body they can find. This accounts for one member of a family's being so entirely different from the rest, in both looks, tastes, disposition and habits. If these differences are of a negative character such a one may be a "black sheep" and often without any affection for his parents or brothers and sisters. Often such a one may find greater friendships, love and closer ties with the members of another family in which it should have incarnated, were it not prevented by karmic or other reasons. Such a one simply did not belong to the first family group in the past and so does not "fit in" to it now.

STAGES OF INCARNATION

The incarnation is a progressive affair, one stage following another. The Soul may have been overshadowing the mother for some time, but makes direct contact at the time of conception. At the time of conception the forces of the physical permanent atom are then encountered. These modify both the etheric double or pattern-body and the physical body. This modification brings over so much of the last personality—we would say at least half—that it modifies the family heredity so markedly that, as we have said before, if anyone could see a picture of you in your last life he would instantly recognize you. This accounts for the marked differences in appearance—body, color of hair and eyes, etc.—of the children of the same parents. Otherwise they should be as alike as peas in a pod as they all have the same family heredity and environment. The next major stage of incarnation is at the time of "quickening." The next stage is at the first breath; the next at 7 years and at 12 years. Thus the Soul is not fully incarnated until puberty when the power to create is present, approximately from 10 to 14, according to climate, race, etc.

LENGTH OF INCARNATION SET

You usually incarnate for a definite term of years or the time judged necessary to accomplish the program of attainment you have laid out. You therefore come with a store of vitality to last for that period approximately. This is generally recognized in the expression "his time had come" or "his time was up," etc. But if the cycle you have set is abnormally cut short by war, accident or murder, you may return immediately without ascending into the higher realms, to live out the balance of your cycle. In this case such an incarnation will be a short one. For instance, if your intended cycle was planned for 60 years and you were killed at 20, if you decided to incarnate at once it would be only for the 40 year balance of the cycle of 60 years that was cut short. Hence you would probably live only forty years.

DEATH IN CHILDHOOD

If the Soul plans the length of its incarnation, some persons ask, why it should incarnate for only a few years and die in early childhood. There are several reasons for this. Often the Soul did not need to incarnate at that period but did so because of the intense longing of the mother and the desire of the Soul to comfort her. Sometimes a somewhat advanced Soul comes to lift the mother's thoughts to higher things. Often the whole life of worldly-minded parents is changed to a more spiritual one after a short visit of a more advanced Soul as their child. The short incarnation was like the visit of an angel.

Perhaps in the past the Soul refused—by abortion or other-wise—to give a body to some Soul who desired to incarnate, and so must learn what it means to desire incarnation and be prevented through the destruction of the body through which it wished to be born. If a mother's resentment against mother-hood attracts a low, undeveloped Soul, the fight among such Souls for possession of the body may cause it to abort or be still-born or die soon after birth. Again, an advanced Soul may find inharmony in the family and environment too great for its sensitive body to endure, and so it has to withdraw in early childhood. Remember that the Soul is not an infant when it incarnates, but is at the full stage of unfoldment and maturity its many incarnations have produced. It is only the body that is an infant.

TIME BETWEEN INCARNATIONS

When the planned attainment is accomplished you usu-ally simply withdraw during sleep and the body dies without disease or accident. But if the life-cycle is cut short by condi-tions beyond control — such as war, pestilence or uncontributed accident — you may incarnate directly from the lower astral within a few weeks, months or years, sometimes through the same mother.[3] But, as we have said elsewhere: "Those who do reincarnate without entering the higher realms are less well equipped for their new Earth life, just as a child who leaves school before his education is completed is more or less handi-capped by his lack of advanced training."[4] Also, in the case of quick reincarnation, if the old astral body has not disintegrated before the new incarnation, it may attach itself to the new personality as a "dweller" or incubus.[4]

As every mother must be open to the astral to give incar-nation to the overshadowing Soul, if she is sensitive she may recognize who it is who wishes to incarnate, and even give him the name desired. She may also be impressed with the Soul's chief object in incarnating and so train and prepare him for it.

Thus the time between incarnations varies greatly, from —

---

[4] *Realms of the Living Dead*, Curtiss, 91-85.

in exceptional cases—a few months to thousands of years. The general average is said to be from 200 to 1500 years. As we personally have always been anxious to help humanity our own average has been about 150 to 200 years. In our investigation we encountered one astral teacher who claimed that she was an old Atlantean teacher who had refused to incarnate for over 20,000 years so that she might continue to give her teachings to humanity through various mediums all down through the ages. Instead of incarnating from time to time and progressing, her mighty will and her intense desire to help humanity held her voluntarily earth-bound in the higher astral. So instead of teaching advanced concepts of the laws of life, she continued to give out the same old Atlantean concepts.

As a rule the more advanced one is, the longer he remains out of incarnation, unless there is some special reason—such as helping humanity in some special way, such as spiritual teaching, etc.—that brings him back earlier. Some advanced Masters have had to wait for centuries for the proper planetary and racial cycles and karmic conditions to arrive which would permit them to accomplish their mission.

SPECIAL INCARNATIONS

There are special messengers who incarnate to teach or rule or warn, like the prophets, or to intervene to save a nation like Joan of Arc. There are other great Souls whose mission requires them to remain on Earth for exceptionally long periods, such as the Masters of Wisdom of India and the Masters of Egypt who are at the head of the Egyptian Hierarchy of the Great White Lodge of Masters who usually remain in incarnation in certain Egyptian temples for 300 years or more.

Then there are the Celestial Beings, the Avatars, like Melchizedek, Krishna and Jesus. They incarnated not through the gate of ordinary birth, but phenomenally. Such Avatars incar-

nate at the beginning of every Great Age (2160 years) to give
out the teachings of that Age. Or they incarnate "whenever
there is a decline in virtue and an insurrection of vice and
injustice in the world; and thus I incarnate from age to age for
the preservation of the just, the destruction of the wicked, and
the establishment of righteousness."[5] The cycle for another
such celestial incarnation is now at hand and the great event
may take place at any time after the Battle of Armageddon.[6]

TIMES OF VARIOUS CLASSES

According to Dr. Frank Crane the time between incarnations
varies as follows: "Unskilled laborers from 60 to 100 years.
Skilled laborers from 100 to 200 years. The Bourgeoise from
200 to 300 years. And so on up to the highest class of 'gentle-
men farmers' and professional men who remain out from 600
to 1000 years or more."

Dr. Crane gives the following as probable: "Epictetus re-
turned as Ralph Waldo Emerson; Cicero as Gladstone; Julius
Caesar as Theodore Roosevelt, (some say as Mussolini);
Ashoka of India as Col Olcott; Hypatia of Alexandria as
Giordano Bruno and then as Mme. Blavatsky; Alfred the Great
as Queen Victoria; William the Conqueror as Lord Kitchener;
Virgil as Lord Tennyson; Pythagoras as Koot Hoomie; Francis
Bacon was Robertus in the 16th century, Hunyadi Janos in the
15th and Christian Rosencreuz in the 14th century."

We do not give the above as authoritative but as one writer's
estimate. But it is suggestive.

Since animals do not have individualized souls, but are
limited expressions of their Group Soul in the higher astral,[7]
they do not reincarnate individually, although they do have
varying lengths of life in the astral world after death.[7] But if
a pet animal has been given a great amount of attention and
training, and has had much love lavished on it, it has absorbed
so much of your human atoms from your physical, astral, men

---

[5] *The Bhagavad Gita*, Chapter iv.
[6] For details see *The Philosophy of War*, Curtiss, chapter vii.
[7] For details see *Letters from the Teacher, I*, Curtiss, 223-226. Also *Realms of the Living Dead*, Curtiss, 45.

tal and spiritual bodies that it is to that extent partly humanized. In other words, you have "ensouled" it with a part—the emanations—of yourself. It therefore may reincarnate with you, even more than once in your present life time. For instance, when a dog suddenly sees a stranger and persistently follows him and attaches himself to him, the dog may have simply recognized a former master.[8] No doubt the above is the reason Mohammed declared that some animals enter heaven, meaning an after-death existence.

---

[8] *When Your Animal Dies*, Barbanell

IN THE NEW TESTAMENT. OBJECTIONS ANSWERED

PART III

> "The first centuries of Christianity found reincarnation still the prevailing creed, as in all previous ages. . . . It enlarges Christianity to grander capacity than it has hitherto known, and so furnishes at once an inspiring religion for the loftiest spiritual aspiration, a most satisfactory philosophy for the intellect, and the strongest basis for practical nobility of conduct."
>
> *Reincarnation*, Walker, 225, 318.

TRUTH IS A MANY-SIDED JEWEL which can be possessed only through understanding. In every age certain rays of universal truth are flashed to the world, but colored by the current stage of civilization and interpreted according to the popular race-thought of the times. To grasp a truth itself you must rise above racial and sectarian concepts and prejudices and get the cosmic concept of the ray of truth under consideration. Then you will see that it is only a colored aspect of the truth itself, just as the colors of the spectrum are not light itself, only colored aspects of the one white light. The *Bible* is the ray of spiritual light for the western world. To understand it properly you must rise above sectarian interpretations and get the cosmic concept of its presentation of truth.

A CHRISTIAN DOCTRINE

One objection which some narrow-minded people make to reincarnation, which prevents them from even studying it, is that it is not sanctioned by the Church and is therefore not a Christian doctrine. This, of course, is not true, and such a statement only reveals the speaker's ignorance of Church history. In reality, reincarnation is the philosophical salvation of

Christianity. Without it the scheme of universal salvation fails, for God has had the vast majority of mankind incarnate in races which never heard of Jesus or the Christian doctrines. Hence, according to certain sects, they are thereby condemned to hell-fire.[1] Even in so-called Christian countries, few really live up to the Christian teachings, so only those few are theoretically "saved." But with Reincarnation, no matter how great the failures or how great the evil generated in one life, none are condemned to "everlasting punishment," but will have many more chances to redeem their mistakes and continue their advance.

CHURCH FATHERS

To say that reincarnation is not a Christian doctrine is to ignore the teachings of the most distinguished authorities of the early Church Fathers. For more than *three hundred years after* Jesus' specific teaching on the subject it was distinctly preached as the only means of reconciling the existence of suffering and inherited deformities and diseases with a just and merciful Cod.

Justin Martyr (100-167 A.D.), the greatest authority on Church history up to the middle of the second century, expressly speaks of the Soul's inhabiting more than one human body. St Clement, Bishop of Alexandria (150-215 A.D.), who brought the culture and philosophy of the Greeks to the Christian Church and who was the teacher of Origen, also held and taught this doctrine. St. Gregory of Nyssa (329-389) said: "It is absolutely necessary that the Soul should be healed and purified, and if this does not take place during its life on Earth, it must be accomplished in *future lives*." St Jerome (340-420 A.D.), in his *Epistle to Avitus*, held the doctrine was taught as a mystery in the early Church. Arnobius Rufinus (345-410 A.D.) in his letter to Anastasius says: "We die many times," and that this doctrine was common among the early

---

[1] See "The Doctrine of Hell Fire," *The Voice of Isis*, Curtiss.

Church Fathers. St Augustine (354-430 A.D.), Bishop of Hippo, in his great *Opera i*, 294, also held the doctrine, and in his *Confessions*, i, 6, asks: "Did I not live in another body, or somewhere else, before entering my mother's womb?"

ORIGEN ADAMANTIVE

And Origen (185-254 A. D.), who is called, "The most distinguished and most influential of all the theologians of the ancient church. . . . the father of the Church's science. . . . the founder of the Church's theology. . . . finding an intellectual expression and philosophical basis for Christianity. . . . besides whose essays later teachings are like school boys' essays," held firmly to reincarnation. In *De Principis* he says that in the body each Soul enjoys that lot which is most exactly suited to his previous habits. In *Contra Celsum* he asks: "Is it not more in conformity with reason that every Soul. . . . is introduced into a body. . . . according to its deserts *and former actions*?" In this way alone he thought the justice of God could be defended.

It has been said that his opinions were condemned by the Church, but such condemnation was made by the Patriarch of Constantinople—instigated by Emporer Justinius—at a local synod in 543 A.D. and not by the Fifth General Council in 553 A.D., at which time the question was not even raised. So the doctrine has never been officially anathematized or declared heretical by the Christian Church, in spite of the fact that "Emperor Justinius condemned Origen by an imperial edict which later was confirmed by Pope Vigilius."

OBJECTIONS ANSWERED

The reason for belief in reincarnation by the Church Fathers is found in the Bible itself; for to say that it is not taught in the *New Testament* is to ignore what Jesus specifically stated, as well as several other passages where it is either re-

ferred to or implied. The passages which are most convincing
and which forestall all argument are Jesus' own direct and
specific statements that John the Baptist was the reincarnation of Elias.

WHO WAS JOHN THE BAPTIST?

In *Matthew, xvii*, 10-13, we read: "Elias truly shall first
come and restore all things ("fulfill the ancient teachings,"
Lamsa). But I say unto you, *That Elias is come already*, and
they knew him not. . . . then the disciples understood that he
spake unto them of John the Baptist." We find the same statement in chapter xi, 14. Referring to John the Baptist, Jesus said:
"And if ye will receive it, *this is Elias* which was for to come."
As John's teachings spread it was generally recognized, "That
it is Elias. And others said, That it is a prophet" (reincarnated).
Mark vi, 15.

Some writers try to get around these specific statements by
saying that John fulfilled the prophecy quoted in *Luke, i, 17*,
by coming "in the spirit and power of Elias," only. Of course
John had the spirit and power of Elias because he brought over
all his previous attainments and powers as innate qualities with
which he was born, as we have already explained. Others say
that John could not have been Elias because when he appeared
with Moses at the Transfiguration (*Matth. xvii, 3*) he appeared
as Elias and not as John. This is easily explained by the fact
that after death you usually prefer to assume the likeness of
the greatest personality you have manifested in your major
incarnations, as the personality and station in life assumed
during the minor incarnations is relatively insignificant.

Since we have estimated that you bring back at least half
the characteristics of your previous personality, we would
naturally expect this rule to apply to Elias, and so we find it.
"He was a hairy man, and girt with a girdle of leather about

his loins." (*II Kings, i, 8*). And he resided largely in the wilderness. Likewise, "Came John the Baptist, preaching in the wilderness. . . . And the same John had his raiment of camel's hair, and a leather girdle about his loins." (*Matth. iii, 1-4*). "And he shall go before him in the spirit and power of Elias." (*Luke, i, 17*). Why "in the spirit and power of Elias" rather than any other prophet *if he were not Elias*? Thus 1000 years after Elias, John the Baptist came with the same type of personality and *with the same habits* that he had as Elias, and prophesying the coming of the Lord just as did Elias (*Malachi iv, 5; Luke iii, 4*). The fact that John denied that he was Elias (*John i, 21*) merely proves that we do not remember our past incarnations.

REINCARNATION WELL KNOWN

The doctrine was so well known that when Herod heard of Jesus' fame as a preacher he naturally concluded that "This is John the Baptist (whom Herod had already beheaded); he is risen from the dead." Likewise reincarnation was so well known to the disciples that when Jesus asked them: "Who do men say that I the Son of Man am?" they all began to guess who He might have been in a previous incarnation. "Some say thou art John the Baptist; some Elias; and others Jeremias, or one of the prophets." (*Matth. xvi, 13-14*).

Familiarity with reincarnation by the disciples is again clearly shown when they asked Jesus about the man who was born blind. "Master, who did this sin, *this man*, or his parents, that he was born blind?" (*John ix, 2*). It is reasonable to imagine that the parents may have committed some sin because of which the son was born blind, but how could the man *himself* have sinned *before* he was born? Could he have sinned in heaven before his birth? Obviously not. Therefore the implication is plain that he must have sinned in a previous life to be born blind in this life.

JONAH AS PETER

Jesus called Peter "Simon Bar-jona" (*Matth. xvi, 17*), meaning "son of Jonah," although Peter was not a lineal descendant
of Jonah. This plainly referred to a previous incarnation as
Jonah. This is confirmed by the marked *similarity in character* and *habits* of the two personalities. For Peter was the
same type of obstinate, combative, self-assertive and impulsive character as Jonah. Peter was so impulsive that he cut
off the right ear of the high priest's servant. Also he was so
impressed by the materialization of Moses and Elias to Jesus
on the mount of transfiguration that immediately he wanted to
establish three tabernacles in commemoration of so remarkable
an event. When he was accused of being a follower of Jesus,
he was afraid and denied Jesus thrice and then fled and wept
bitterly. Likewise Jonah was afraid and fled when ordered to
go to Ninevah.

When Jesus told Nicodemus: "Except a man be born again
he cannot see the kingdom of God," Nicodemus showed both
his lack of knowledge of reincarnation and also of Jesus' spiritual meaning (*John, iii, 3*). But this lack of understanding of the
meaning of "born again" (*yalad*) was only natural as he spoke
only the Chaldean Aramaic, like all the Jews of Judea, while
Jesus spoke the Galilean Aramaic. Jesus was so astonished
at Nicodemus' lack of knowledge of both reincarnation and
spiritual birth that He exclaimed: "Art thou a master (teacher)
of Israel, and knowest not these things?" (*John, iii, 10*).

QUEEN OF SHEBA

In *Matthew xii, 41-2* we have two verses which have no
relevant meaning except in the light of reincarnation. "The men
of Nineveh shall rise up in judgment with this generation, and
shall condemn it: because they repented at the preaching of
Jonas; and, behold, a greater than Jonas is here." How could

the men of Nineveh rise and condemn that generation unless they were again in incarnation, as was also Jonas as Peter? Also, "The Queen of the South (Sheba) shall rise up in judgment with this generation, and shall condemn it: for she came from the utttermost parts of the earth (Ethiopia) to hear the wisdom of Solomon; and, behold, a greater than Solomon is here." To thus condemn that generation the Queen of Sheba must also have been in incarnation like the men of Nineveh, and condemned it for the same reason.

Again, we find Jesus saying that those who have attained full Mastery, "which shall be accounted worthy to obtain that world, and the resurrection from the dead (or from the necessity of reincarnating) . . . . *Neither can they die any more*: for they are equal to the angels; and are the children of God, being the children of the resurrection." (*Luke xx, 35-6*).

In *Acts xv, 16*, we are told that Jesus would return and rebuild His tabernacle or the "throne of David," on the former ruins, as promised to Mary at the time of her conception. To confirm this we are told: "Bethlehem. . . . out of thee shall he come forth unto me that is to be ruler in Israel: whose *goings forth* (incarnations) have been from old, from everlasting." (*Micah,v,2,3.*)

In *Revelation, iii, 12*, we are told: "Him that overcometh (or has finished his incarnations) I will make a pillar in the temple of my God, and he shall *go no more out*." That is, will no longer need to descend or "go out" into incarnation again.

Another passage that is frequently overlooked in this connection is found in *St. John, viii, 53-54*. Therein Jesus plainly states that He was in incarnation during the days of Abraham and saw him personally. When the Jews asked Him: "Whom makest thou thyself?" Jesus replied: "Your father Abraham rejoiced to see my day: and he say it, and was glad." Then said the Jews, "Thou art not yet fifty years old, and thou hast seen Abraham?" Jesus said unto them, "Verily, verily, I say unto you, (even) Before Abraham was, I am."

Thus we see that reincarnation is not only *taught specifically* by Jesus Himself, but is in the background and is assumed in all His general teachings.

OBJECTIONS ANSWERED

1. "Why cannot I remember?"

Probably the objection most often raised to reincarnation is the fact that you do not remember your past lives.[2] Since progress depends upon your forgetting the details of your earlier steps, your progress here would be tremendously handicapped if you remembered all the events of your past lives. In fact, it is providential that your memory of past enmities, hatreds, prejudices and injustices is forgotten, so that when you associate with those with whom they were formed you can start afresh and give them and yourself a chance to adjust the inharmony without your opposition. Also, since if the recalling of past mistakes and faults in this life makes you sad and remorseful, remembering those of past lives would be overwhelmingly discouraging.

The reason you do not remember past lives is that your parents have furnished you with a brand new brain, and naturally it records only that to which it responds *in this life*. And since you did not have this brain in a past life you cannot expect it to record the vibrations of a past life which it never experienced.

For students to find out who they were often so diverts their attention from their present-day duties that their present incarnation is greatly hampered. Do not look to the past for guidance, but to the Christ-within who knows all and therefore what is best for you. No matter what you have been in the past *you are now the embodiment of all you have been*. You are here to live *this life* and learn its lessons *here and now*.

---

[2] For details see "Memory of Past Lives" in *Letters from the Teacher*, Curtiss, ii, 269.

So do not waste time dreaming about what you might have been, but live in the ever-present now. It is not what you have been but *what you are now* that counts. What use you make of your opportunities in this life will determine what you *will* be, and also your conditions, in your next incarnation. *Your future life will be what you make it now.*

Only when you advance to a point where, through spiritual growth, you can respond to spiritual forces, can you tap your Soul-memory, wherein the experiences of all lives are recorded, and remember your past lives. Sometimes in an emergency a flash or picture of some particular incident in the past is given you in a dream, vision or intuition to warn, encourage or otherwise help you to conquer a test in which you failed in a previous life.[1]

2. "Does not heredity account for all?"

Not so, for heredity transmits bodily characteristics only. If mental characteristics *seem* to be transmitted it is only because all the children are necessarily furnished brains having the same *family heredity* which naturally modifies the expression of the mind manifesting through them. Heredity does not account for many things, such as the great divergences from the family type, or for the different color of hair or eyes among children of the same parents. Nor does it account for the possession of unusual talents or genius where there is no trace of them in the family tree. If heredity were the dominating factor the Dione quintuplets would be as alike as peas in a pod, as they were born of the same parents, at the same time and in the same environment. While breeding is transmitted by heredity, genius is not.

3. "Does not determinism or the influence of environment account for all?"

Environment has an influence but it is a *minor* one. If it were the dominant factor it could not be transcended. Great men and many others often succeed by transcending all the limitations and influences of determinism in their environments. Hence, if environment can be so easily transcended it is only a *secondary* influence. Lincoln, Franklin, Carnegie, Schwab, Knudsen, Edison and Ford had no formal education yet they each transcended that limitation and have made indelible marks in the world.

4. "I don't want to be someone else."

You always remain *yourself*, even though dressed in a new suit or body which makes you *appear* different, although you still look so much as you did in the last life that anyone would recognize you from a picture of you in the last life.

5. "Would it not separate families and loved ones?"

It would not, for families and loved ones tend to incarnate *together*. Loved ones are brought together sooner or later, often from the ends of the earth. Groups, nations and races also incarnate together because of the ties set up together.

6. "Isn't it unjust to be punished for something you know nothing about?"

You are not. Even in this life you often suffer later in life for faults, sins and mistakes made in youth which you had entirely forgotten and hence know nothing about until they are recalled to your mind. In either case *you are not punished*. You are only reaping the results of your own causing. You are not punished *for* your sins, but *by* their results.

7. "Might I not come back as an animal?"

No. That is not the doctrine of reincarnation. That is the erroneous and misguided doctrine of *transmigration*. It is not possible, because no body below the human shape has the centers and organs that can accommodate a human Soul.

8. "Isn't it a cold and irreligious doctrine?"

It is not a man-made doctrine but a cosmic law. It is taught by nearly all the great religions.

9. "Doesn't it do away with the forgiveness of sins?"

Your sins may be forgiven but you must still reap the outer results of your own creations unless their Karma is neutralized by an *excess* of spiritual attainment or by "the Grace of God."

10. "Doesn't it do away with the atoning blood of the Christ?"

It does not; for the "blood" or the spiritual life-force of the Christ is still the power which must be used to redeem your mistakes and set you free.

11. "Isn't it anti-Christian?"

Not so. Jesus and the early church taught it specifically, as we have already explained,

12. "Wouldn't it take too long to master all Earth conditions?" You have all the time there is, eternity. There is neither any compulsion nor any hurry. You take your own time and can remain out of incarnation as long as you wish.

13. "The Earth is not the only plane on which you can progress. You can advance in the astral world after death here."

You do progress there, but you have to come back and prove that progress by *demonstrating* it in the flesh, the most hampering and hardest condition to manifest in. The Earth is the plane of testing and demonstration. All must be expressed in matter to complete the cycle. The astral is the "Hall of Learning," the physical the "Hall of Redemption and Demonstration."

14. "You can progress on other planets so why do you need to come back to Earth?"

So you can, but you have to come back and *demonstrate* your advance here in matter until you have attained full Mastery here. Your Soul-home may be on another planet, but you must demonstrate your degrees of unfoldment *here*. Those from the Sun are teachers, usually spiritual teachers.

Those from Jupiter have the judicial temperament, judges, etc. Those from Mars are not only warriors but executives, those who get things done. Those from Venus excel in the mothering quality. Those from Mercury are scientists or high intellectuals, etc., but all have to demonstrate their talents here in matter.

15. "A child in the eighth grade doesn't need to come back and start in all over again, forgetting all advance and repeating old lessons."

You do not have to repeat old lessons unless they were not fully learned. If their qualities were built into your character they will appear in the new personality as inherent faculties. You start in right where you left off.

16. "Spirit Guides say they know nothing of reincarnation."

Since you associate with people of like interests and advancement after death, just as you do here, if none of your friends or those who are guides now were interested in reincarnation while here, it is not likely they would be interested afterward unless they made a special study of it after passing over. We have induced many guides to look into it and they have all been thoroughly convinced after contacting the higher teachers over there, and have taught it at their seances ever since.

17. "If I am tired of earth conditions do I have to come back?"

You do not have to until you wish to. You can remain out as long as you wish. (Remember the Atlantean teacher who had been out for 20,000 years!) When you have learned all the lessons life here can teach, and have demonstrated all your spiritual qualities you need not return.

18. "If rebirth perfects the Soul, why is humanity still so imperfect, and where are the perfected ones?"

For the masses the process is a slow one, like evolution, because they make no *definite efforts* to conquer and progress.

The advanced Souls who have completed their experiences and work on Earth still carry on in the higher realms, as they have no need to remain here unless they come back to help the less advanced. They are the great spiritual leaders.

19. "With regeneration, translation and the ascension, is rebirth necessary?"

Regeneration and the ascension come not by "decrees," but only through the mastery of all earth conditions and the transmutation and *spiritualization* of the flesh through the radiations of the indwelling Christ-power. If this is really your last incarnation and you are taking the last steps necessary for the ascension you will be so spiritually advanced that you will lead such a beautiful life that you will be known as a saint practically from childhood. If you have not led such a life naturally and instinctively then this is not your last life here and you are therefore not ready to make the ascension.

20. "So many claim to have been kings and queens or of exalted rank or position."

If they were, then the *qualities* which made them great in the past *will show* in their character *now*. Many in the past so identified their interest and admiration with a great character that they brought over an intense admiration which is aroused by a picture or any reference to the great personage. According to the claims made, many were the Virgin Mary, Julius Caesar, Napoleon, etc., but unless they can demonstrate the *qualities* of the great ones they claim to have been they are mistaken.

21. "Is there any scientific, factual proof?"

There are now a great number of physical proofs, cases in which the reincarnation has been *proved* and *legally acknowledged* as we will record herein.

It should be remembered that science is not infallible, but varies its teachings from age to age. It once taught that the

Earth was flat; that the sun revolved around it; that there could be no light without heat; that atoms were composed of matter, etc., all of which have subsequently been proved to be erroneous.

GROWTH DEMANDS EXPANSION

Since you grow through experiences—which bring happiness or suffering—and through the expression of the wisdom learned, the continual expansion of your unfolding powers requires a constant development of the body through which they are expressed. But the limits of growth in one personality are soon reached, and your further progress would be limited if you were confined to one body.

DEATH A RELEASE

Death is, therefore, a welcome release from a worn-out and out-grown body. It enables you to continue the unfoldment and expression of your Spiritual Self by reincarnating in a new and more nearly perfect body which will better express your continued expansion of consciousness.

THE RHYTHM OF LIFE

Death thus acquires a new and deeper significance when we regard it no longer as the end of your only life on Earth, but as part of the continually recurring rhythm of eternal progress, as inevitable, as natural and as benevolent as when we die to earth consciousness during sleep. Death leaves youth behind as sunset leaves the dawn. But both will return in their due cycle to give you a new day in which to continue your progress.

SCIENTIFIC EVIDENCE AND PHYSICAL PROOFS

PART IV

"Great hypotheses have always preceded demonstrations
and verifications. . . . There exists an hypothesis which is
in accord with all the ideas of modern science, and which
explains all the obscure phenomena of normal, abnormal,
supra-normal and even pathological psychology. This
same hypothesis overthrows, decides, difficulties of the
moral and even of the metaphysical order, which, since
the beginning of the human race, have paraded themselves
before the conscience and intelligence."

Reincarnation, Geley, 51, 42.

SINCE THE SOUL-MEMORY of past lives is impressed upon the subconscious mind in this life during the first 21 to 48 months, many children have distinct memories of the past. And since their minds are not crowded with memories of this life, the memories of the past are just as vivid as anything in this life. Hence children should not be laughed at or be accused of "wild imagination" or of telling fibs or be made to suppress them when relating such memories. Later in life the mind becomes so filled with reactions to present-day conditions that the memories of the past become overlaid and buried in the deeper layers of the subconscious. The ancient Egyptians knew enough to pay attention to such memory-recoveries of children. They analyzed them, allowed for the exaggeration of imagination and often thus learned truths that guided them in the education and up-bringing of the child.

CHILDREN'S SAYINGS

One little girl of five, astonished her mother by suddenly remarking: "Mummy, isn't it funny that you didn't know me when I was a grown up young lady? You never were my mother before." Another child said: "I grew up old in heaven before I was born." After being rebuked for a fault another child explained: "You stop! You never dared talk like that to me when I was grown up!" Every little while another child would cry: "I want my two babies." When quizzed about them she said: "I had two babies just alike and God took them away. But He said I could have them when I was grown up again." Attempts to satisfy her with twin dolls were in vain. She insisted: "No, I want my really, truly live babies."

A student recently wrote us: "Beginning at the age of four, and on through my childhood, hearing music invariably made me see the same picture: A very large gray stone house (about the size of the White House) set far back from the road in a beautiful park of huge trees. The house could be plainly seen because the trees were very tall and with no low branches. As far as I could see the ground was level and covered with thick, closely cut grass. I did not think much about the house at the time, but as I look back on the picture the building was a large mansion of classical simplicity, with no portico and the wide doorway was only one step above the ground. I did not enter the house, but I could see it plainly in the distance through the enormous trees and I can see it just as plainly today.

To the right of the walk, which led straight to the front door, and in the midst of a circle of trees, a band played stirring music. The musicians were seated, excepting the leader, and all wore scarlet uniforms with gold braid. There were quite a number of 'grown-ups' walking around, some standing or sitting in groups, but I was the only child present. I can still see my little sheer white dress and light blue sash; my golden curls (and I really had them when I was a baby!) were tied with a light blue ribbon to match my sash. White socks and tiny black slippers completed my toilet.

"I can remember so well wondering why everybody there made so much over me. I have no memory of knowing anyone there personally, yet I was not afraid of anyone. Even the musicians and the band leader seemed to try to pay me some special attention. Though I did not understand it and wondered what it was all about, I accepted their admiration gravely and was more dignified at the age of four than I am at sixty one! And my dignity was not confined to this 'dream,' as it was called, for I was in real life a very quiet and thoughtful little child.

"I did not think much about this dream or vision, until I heard music and then the picture was so startlingly clear and vivid that I would cry out to my parents: 'O, tell me *where* is the big gray stone house and *who* are the men that play music under the trees?" My parents tried their best to think of any place we had been that was like the picture I described, but all they could say was that it must have been a dream.

To call it only a dream bothered me greatly. I would exclaim: 'But I *know* I was there!' And I always wanted to find the beautiful green park, the stone house and the wonderful old trees. As I grew older and heard music more frequently, I could hear it without thinking of the dream. Never-the-less, there was quite a thrill in store for me the first time I heard that lovely song from The Bohemian Girl'. . . .

> 'I dreamt that I dwelt in marble halls
> With vassals and serfs at my side
> And of all that dwelt within those walls,
> I was their joy and pride.'

I can't describe how that affected me. . . . it brought back the dream so vividly and by changing a few words it seemed to be my very own song:

'I dreamt I dwelt in gray stone halls
With many kinds friends at my side
And of all that dwelt within those walls,
That I was their joy and pride.'

"As I grew older and became much interested in history, archeology and genealogical research, I have so often felt myself being strongly drawn back to the past and have so frequently felt that I do not belong to this age at all. Though interested in Egypt and the Holy Land, some strong invisible tie seems to bind me to England and Ireland. Though I do not know that I had any Irish ancestors, yet ancient Ireland, as well as my beloved 'Mother Country,' England, keeps pulling me back."

SPEAKING FRENCH ONLY

A mother recently told us: "Our third child, Carol, was different in all her reactions from the first two children. She refused to attempt to speak English and formulated a complete language of her own. I took her to several psychiatrists in the hope that I would discover what caused her speech aversion. They found her to be perfectly normal mentally, but could give no reason for her refusal to attempt to speak English.

This attitude continued *until she was four years of age.* Several months before her birthday I said: 'Carol, let's go for a walk. Go upstairs and get your hat.' She looked at me blithely for awhile and trilled: 'Mais oui, Maman, ou est mon chapeau?' As our only household help had consisted of a good old Virginia mammy, and my journey into French had begun and ended in high school, I was completely taken by surprise. I followed a strong hunch and took Carol to a private kindergarten run by a delightful French woman. Carol joined in the singing of French songs and after a month of joy in an atmosphere peculiarly her own, began to speak English volubly.

She is now twelve years of age and continues to reach back to another life and time, with constant references to the beauty of France and her love for Paris. She said to me the other day: 'You must really go to Paris with me, Monie. It is beautiful. Of course, England is lovely too, but I always liked France much more than England'."

NO EXPLANATION

Merely to say that such spontaneous and detailed memories of places and languages "came from the subconscious mind," when there had been no experience in this life even remotely to suggest them, is to explain nothing unless it can also be shown how such detailed and circumstantial ideas got into the subconscious mind. Their presence in the subconscious cannot be accounted for except as memories of past lives transferred there during the first two years of life, as already described in *Part II* of this series.

PHYSICAL PROOFS

While such memories of children are significant and of presumptive evidence, they are not conclusive *proof* until scientifically corroborated and verified. Fortunately there are a number of such cases which have been scientifically verified and acknowledged and substantiated by evidence produced in court.

Perhaps the most remarkable and thoroughly proved case, which cannot be explained away by imagination, dreaming or telepathy, is that of the 9 year old Hindu girl *Shanti Kumari*, sometimes called Shanti Devi, living in the *Cheera Khana* quarter of Delhi, India. From earliest childhood she insisted that the house was not her home, nor was Delhi her home town. Later she added detail after detail about her former life. She said she was the wife of a cloth merchant by the name of Pandit Kadar Nath Chanbey living at a given address in the village of Muttra, by whom she had had two children.

Her grand uncle, Mr. Bishan Chand, wrote to Pt. Chanbey at the address given and all were astonished to receive a reply from him corroborating the details given in the letter. Later his elder brother visited her at Delhi, was immediately recognized by her as her *Jeth* or elder brother-in-law, and she correctly answered all his questions.

Still later Kedar Nath and his son (now 10 years old) themselves visited her and both were recognized with tears of joy, and she was able to answer the most intimate questions as to the details of their family life so correctly that Kedar Nath said he felt that he was indeed talking to his former wife. She gave detailed descriptions of the clothes and ornaments she had worn, together with a correct description of the closets in which they were kept, and using the idioms of the Muttra dialect which were unknown in Delhi.

IDENTIFIES HOME AND FRIENDS

Later on Shanti Kumari was taken to Muttra where she directed the driver of the *tonga* to the street she had named. There she jumped out and ran up to the correct house.

She identified various members of the family and friends out of a group of more than fifty persons. The aged Brahman whom she greeted as "father-in-law" was indeed the father of Pt. Chanbey whom she recognized as her former husband. She pointed out where there should be a well. Some coverings were removed and the well was found. Shanti Kumari had promised the Dwarkadhish Temple 100 rupees which she had accumulated and hidden under the floor boards in a certain room of her former home. Upon removing the boards, to the astonishment of all, the money was found.

The facts of this test are vouched for both by her former husband, mother, son, father-in-law, and also by the distinguished independent investigator, Lal Desh Bandhu Gupta, managing director of the leading newspaper of Delhi, *The*

Daily Tej, Pandit Neki Bam Shanna, the leader of the National Congress Party, and Prof. Indra Sen, the distinguished psychist of Delhi University, who represented the All-India Psychists' Association. This case was also reported by James A. Miller, foreign correspondent for *The Associated Press*, adding that Mahatma Gandi had invited Kumari Shanti Devi to his seminary at Wardha. Since there can be no doubt about the facts, this case must be regarded as *a physical proof* of reincarnation.

MONSUR ATRASH

Another physical proof of reincarnation is the case of Monsur Atrash of the Jebel Druz in Syria. Some time after he married the beautiful girl Ummrumman, he was killed in a raid. At the hour of his death—afterward verified—a boy named Najib Abu Faray was born in the mountains of Lebanon, hundreds of miles away. Reaching the age of 20 without having left his native mountains, by accident he was taken to the mountain home of Monsur Atrash. As soon as he reached the mountain he exclaimed: "I must be in a dream! I have seen all these places before; they are more familiar than my native mountains."

When he came to the village where Monsur Atrash had lived he said: "This is my village, and my home is up a certain street on a certain corner." He walked through the queer twisting streets, straight to the house of Monsur Atrash, went to a walled-up window, had the bricks torn out and found a bag of money he remembered having put there before he went on the raid in which Monsur Atrash was killed.

Later he was taken to some vineyards of the Atrash family about which there were disputed boundaries. He pointed out the boundaries he had laid down as Monsur Atrash, and *a court of law* accepted them as correct. He had now given so many proofs of his identity that he was recognized *by the children of Monsur Atrash as their father*, and he received ten

camel-loads of grain as a present from the Atrash family.
Where a court of the land, after full investigation, *officially
recognizes the reincarnation* of the same person, no further
proof is necessary.

ALEXANDRINE SAMONA

On March 15th, 1910, Alexandrine Samona died at the age
of 5. Three nights later her mother dreamed of her saying:
"Mamma, do not cry any more. . . . I shall return as small as
that," showing a little embryo. Three nights later the dream
was repeated. A few days later while the parents were holding
some typtological mediumistic sittings, Alexandrine commu-
nicated the statement that she would be reborn through her
mother "before Christmas." She also said that her father's
sister, Jeanne, who died at the age of 15, would incarnate with
her, but if the mother did not cease grieving she would give
them greatly depleted bodies. This shows the powerful effect
the mother's emotions can have on the children she is carrying.
Jeanne also stated that Alexandrine would be reborn "at least
a little more beautiful."

On November 23rd the mother gave birth to twin girls. The
two differed perceptibly in height, complexion and figure. The
smaller was a faithful copy of Alexandrine at the time she was
first born; and extraordinarily, she had hyperemia in her left
eye, a slight running in the right ear, and a slight irregularity
of the face *all quite identical* with that which Alexandrine had
at the time of her first birth.

PRINCESS LEI KAHANNI

As a child, Princess Lei Kahanni of Hawaii insisted that
she had been the mother of a beautiful baby boy and had
lived on a large estate near a lake and a marsh. She also
described the various rooms of the mansion and their fur-
nishings. She was so insistent that her parents jokingly began
to look for such a place. After some time a place was found

about which there was a tale of a beautiful lady and her baby who had mysteriously disappeared years ago. It was haunted by a woman's screams and the wail of a baby.

When the Princess was brought to the spot she recognized it as her former home. This caused much excitement, as none of the family had ever been in that part of the country. The little girl led them to a room in which there was a picture of a baby, and said: "That is my baby. I was married to one of two brothers, but was told that I would never live to enjoy my married bliss. When my husband went away on long trips his brother made love to me, but I repulsed him. . . . One moonlight night I was out near the lake with the baby when he came after me, seemingly intoxicated. My resistance drove him into frenzy. He grabbed my baby and strangled it and threw it into the lake. . . . then choked me to death and threw my body into the quicksand by the lake." Later the details of this child's weird story were corroborated by the history of the place. Another physical proof of reincarnation.

MME. LOURE RAYNAUD

At the beginning of the last century Mme. Loure Raynaud remembered, from childhood, that she had lived before and gave detailed descriptions of her former home and the conditions of her death. She said she was not buried in the local cemetery, but in a church some distance away. Forty-five years later, on her first visit to Genoa, she located her former home and research proved that a young lady of her description had died in that house and had been buried in the church Mme. Raynaud had described.

ANNA KONNERSREUTH

The case of Anna Konnersreuth, the young Austrian peasant girl, is also a most remarkable one. At certain feast days of the church she would show the stigmata of the wounds of Jesus when on the cross, and they would bleed freely on each occasion. On these occasions she would also speak the Galilean dialect of the Aramaic language which Jesus spoke. She would also describe various incidents of Jesus' life, which were filled with eye-witness details. As she was an uneducated peasant girl, naturally she had never heard a word of Aramaic, still less the peculiar Galilean dialect, nor was she under psychic control of some disembodied Galilean. So it is evident that her descriptions and use of the language were memories brought over from a Galilean incarnation.

Reincarnation is therefore sustained not only by tradition, reason, logic and the testimony of the greatest minds throughout the ages, but is *definitely proved by* those who have amply substantiated their claims.

PLAN YOUR FUTURE LIFE

A practical understanding of the Law of Rebirth, and of the interval between incarnations while in the higher realms,[1] is most advantageous for planning your life here and hereafter, as well as cultivating happiness, developing love and brotherhood, and protecting yourself from misery and suffering here and now. Ignorance of this law is one of the prime factors in the growth of atheism, crime, racketeering and totalitarian despotisms. Such ignorance also contributes to self-indulgence, lack of discrimination and callousness to the suffering and fate of others. Thus the world is sinking deeper into the unhappiness and miseries brought about by materialism and the ignoring of spiritual values.

How different the life based on the Law of Rebirth! Then the whole outlook is optimistic and encouraging. Life opens out as a beneficent path of eternal progress onward and upward. Even though the forces of evil are great and multiply themselves tremendously through ignorance of this basic law of life and progress, nevertheless there can be no doubt that the *fundamental powers of the universe are infinitely good.*

---

[1] For details see Realms of the *Living Dead*, Curtiss.

And although humanity is now passing through the darkest hour before the New Day of light, love and brotherhood, the *supremacy of good* will *ultimately overcome* the evil, for *good is positive and immortal* while evil is *negative and transitory.* The darkness of the night is chill and depressing, but it is sure to be dispelled by the light and warmth of the rising Sun. And an understanding of the Law of Rebirth assures us that *the New Day* will dawn.

Belief in reincarnation is not essential to your spiritual growth nor to your "salvation" after death. So, if it does not appeal to your reason and common sense as the only explanation that covers all the otherwise inexplicable events of life, and if it does not appeal to your heart as the only solution of the many seeming injustices of life, then just put it aside and do not give it a second thought. *You will come back just the same* whether you believe in it or not.

ITS MOTIVE POWER GREAT

As a Scotch professor has said: "The ethical leverage of the doctrine is immense. Its motive power is great. It reveals a magnificent background to the present life, with its contradictions and disasters, as the prospect of immortality opens up an illimitable foreground. It binds together the past and the future in one ethical series of causes and effects. . . . With peculiar emphasis it proclaims the survival of moral individuality and *personal identity* along with the final adjustment of external conditions to the internal state of the Soul." This explanation of life restores the continuity of the Past, Present and Future of human evolution and clearly emphasizes the vital truth of your own responsibility for your present conditions and also for what they will be in your future incarnations.

A GLORIOUS PROSPECT

The spectacle of the glorious unfoldment of all your god-like spiritual powers through repeated lives, however dormant those powers may be now, presents a vision magnificent and encouraging beyond description. And it more grandly approaches the sublime ideal of human perfection than any other conception of the ultimate manifestation of God in man, the radiant outshining of the Real or Spiritual Self of you through your purified and perfected personality.

"Be worthy of death; and so learn to live
That every incarnation of thy Soul
In varied realms, and worlds and planes
Shall be one more step toward thy goal."

www.ingramcontent.com/pod-product-compliance
Lightning Source LLC
Chambersburg PA
CBHW060709030426

42337CB00017B/2813